Rusty Engineering Management

Rusty Engineering Management

Robert Escriva

Printed in the United States of America.

ISBN 978-1-7376519-9-4 paperback

Independently Published by Robert Escriva,
San Francisco, California, USA

Many people have helped me to get where I am today.
I am grateful to them.

As One Mind

There's something that all productive organizations do: They move as one mind.

That's to say that they make decisions and align themselves so that they can take on external stimulus without internal struggle. Successful startups, large corporations, and the military all exhibit this to some degree. The ability to react quickly and in unison.

There's a reason the Army Corps of Engineers and the National Guard are often dispatched to deal with disasters at home and abroad: They react quickly and are conditioned to execute on orders from above. What starts with, "Deal with the hurricane's damage," gets passed down the chain of command and eventually becomes individual orders to people with no direct reports who may be instructed e.g. to pass out emergency rations. At each level, the individual—and there is just one—breaks down their order or orders into direct orders to their subordinates. The subordinates do this in turn. What starts as a river of a problem at the top of the chain of command becomes a complex delta of tributaries, each contributing to a solution.

In a startup, this manifests as the ability to pivot and take on new business prospects quickly, dealing with the problems that arise with speed. New problems arise and flow up the org chart to the highest level that needs to be aware of or be consulted for a decision. Those below said individual take action; those above remain unaware. Most new objectives make it to a manager. Some make it to a director. Even fewer make it to a VP. By the time an objective makes it to the CEO, the objective has transformed into something appropriate for the level of discussion at which CEOs prefer to make decisions using their tools of the trade.

In the military, they call this a chain of command because the military has the discipline to ensure people report to exactly one individual. Where two individual's orders conflict, the conflict may be escalated to the lowest-rank individual in both chains of command for resolution. The chain of command is literally a chain, and every individual knows exactly where they stand, going all the way up to the commander-in-chief.

In a chain of command, we get something resembling a tree. There is the point where the trunk of the tree meets the ground—the commander in chief. The tree then branches out to top-level individuals who report directly to the commander in chief. From those branches come twigs; yet more reports. And on each twig there are several leaves who have no reports.

But trees are imperfect and undisciplined: In practice the trunk can split and merge—it's rare but it happens. Similarly, non-military organizations with cross-functional modes of operation will have individuals who appear to report to multiple people. This implies that every individual in an organization has someone—or multiple someones—to whom they are accountable.

Usually this accountability relationship is expressed in an org chart, but such a chart doesn't have to, and often does not, match reality. The real definition of the org chart comes in the form of work delegation. When Alice repeatedly delegates to Bob, Bob reports to Alice whether or not the org chart reflects this relationship. Consequently, individuals who work cross-functionally inherently report to multiple people even if they have only a single manager.

The work directly dictates the org chart. Where the two diverge, the work can be seen as ground truth for how people actually work, while the official org chart reflects someone's thoughts about the working relationship between individuals and the priorities of the organization as of the last re-org event. But it can go further than that; the difference between the empirical org chart and the official org chart can be used to drive a re-org to align the structure of the business to its necessary functions. This can even be done programmatically, albeit without emotion or personal considerations relating to how effectively people work together. This is not a problem, however, because people who have a healthy working relationship will see that reflected that in their work output.

Under this model, every organizational objective has an owner. Ownership means the proverbial buck stops with you. No one else cares about a objective that you own if you don't care about it enough to make them care. Ownership confers with it the ability to transfer the owned objective to another individual, or the ability to drop an objective and allow others to completely cancel work pursuant to the objective.

Ownership also comes with one basic property: The ability to delegate the objective to others and make them accountable for the objective. The owner of the objective still cares about the objective, but they are not working on it except to field questions from the individual who they've made accountable for the objective. The accountable individual has complete autonomy on the objective, including to delegate it further.

Accountability brings with it the power to create sub-objectives for the delegated objective. Each of these sub-objectives is owned by the accountable party, but explicitly tied to the objective they are accountable for. They can then delegate these owned objectives to other parties or work on them directly.

This delegation hierarchy makes clear where responsibility for an objective lies. The owner of a objective, and the owner alone, has the ability to drop it or accept it as complete. The accountable party works on the objective directly, and can delegate it in whole or in part to other parties. And accountable parties are partially responsible for the objectives that their objectives descend from.

Ownership flows downward; responsibility flows upward.

There's a mathematical beauty to breaking down objectives along ownership, accountability, and responsibility boundaries. Objectives are owned by the CEO or Commander-in-Chief; every level below that level can only own an objective if it is linked to some *other* objective for which they are personally accountable. In this way, every objective can be traced starting from on high down to the exact work streams necessary to consider it done. Similarly, every objective can be traced starting from the lowest level up to the organizational objective that it directly contributes to in order to increase morale and give a sense of purpose.

In this way, we establish a hierarchy of objectives; through explicit accountability and ownership we can, at all times, verify that the company is working on objectives that align from the leaves to the roots. When everyone is pulling in the same direction, doing the right thing becomes easy. When people are pulling in different directions, the tension is reflected in the ownership of objectives and can be resolved by walking the implicit org chart induced by the objective ownership and delegation. Getting the right owners in the room for making a decision becomes easy.

And a computer can verify that these properties are upheld at all times for everything the organization is on-record as doing. When plans change, the org can rapidly rise to the occasion and verify mechanically that everything still makes sense. In a single move, entire efforts can be abandoned or adjusted to match new organizational-level challenges.

The Buck Stops Here

Ownership means there is no passing of the proverbial buck. There is no one other than the owner who cares about an objective directly; other people only care about an owned objective only as it relates to their own work and incentives.

This definition of ownership is different from the notion of ownership in a traditional organization. In a traditional organization, a manager will divide and distribute the work for individuals and say that they own it. The individual is empowered to make progress on the work and give it back to their manager when its complete. In this book, this traditional notion of ownership is cast as accountability rather than ownership. The individual is not empowered to drop the objective; therefore, they do not own it.

This "drop test" distinguishes between ownership and accountability. Owning an objective confers complete control over the objective. An individual cannot drop something they've been made accountable for because it's not theirs to drop. They can, however, give the objective back with the recommendation that the owner drop it. They are simply borrowing the objective for the time being.

An author of a book that no one knows about owns the book: No one is expecting the book to be delivered, and no one will care if the book gets dropped. Add a publisher to the mix, along with a contract to deliver the book, and the individual no longer owns it—they are accountable to the publisher for delivering the book, and the publisher owns it. When they own the work, an individual can do as they please, and there is no one else who needs to know about the objectives they work on. When they are accountable for the work, they must deliver a finished product that meets someone else's criteria.

Ownership is the ultimate in accountability and responsibility. It's accountability to oneself and society at large for the objective that gets delivered. Without delegation, the objective is solely the owner's responsibility.

For that reason, ownership is a table-stakes game. There is no backstop and there is no one else to do the heavy lifting. There is no pot to fall back upon to play the next hand if this hand's a loss. If the owner fails, there will not be a next hand to play.

Free-form ownership in an organization should be rare and reserved to people whose job literally depends upon their ability to deliver consistently and work in the face of no safety net. We typically refer to these people as Chief, Captain, or General. People whose job it is to own things critical to the business' need and who are literally betting their continued employment on their ability to not royally fuck up.

Ownership is Rare

Unrestricted ownership should be rare within an organization because unrestricted ownership in an organization is chaos.

Here, unrestricted ownership means something very particular: an objective that descends from some other objective is said to be restricted by the objective from which it descends. Unrestricted objectives, then, are free-floating without any parent objective to define them.

If too many individuals own too many unrestricted objectives, there is nothing that ties the organization to a common goal. Sure, people talk and cross-pollinate ideas to stay loosely aligned, but that's not sufficient. When everyone is doing their own thing and are only loosely aligning with others, the organization cannot move fast. If everyone is aligned, moving fast becomes a consequence of daily operations.

For that reason, we add a hierarchy to objectives. Each objective breaks down into one or more sub-objectives that are a prerequisite for considering the work to be complete. In an exemplary organization that's achieved perfect alignment, every objective traces its roots to the objectives set-forth by the leader. The "why" of each objective becomes readily apparent to anyone who can see the picture going up to the root of the organization. Ownership outside the hierarchy is a symptom of friction in the organization and indicates that an individual's priorities are not aligned to the priorities of the person in the org-chart to whom they report.

A nice property that falls out of the way we have framed ownership, accountability, and responsibility is that it's always possible to have every objective descend from objectives set forth by the organization's lead. This is highly desirable: It means that the lead will have a complete picture of the business and be able to make decisions within the framework of thought that works best for them and their reports. They can communicate with their direct reports and know that there are no hidden objectives that are critical to the organization's needs.

In this way, the overheads of running the organization, and the upkeep required to maintain different objectives, percolates up to the leader. Thus, the leader can make decisions about how to adjust operations based upon the complete hierarchy provided to them. Ongoing keep-the-lights-on objectives—often critical when there's engineering involved—become apparent, and the tradeoff between KTLO and new ventures presents itself clearly at all levels. At the CEO's level, objectives may be high level e.g., "Build Widget for new product," and "Keep running the factory for old Gizmo." If the industry is moving rapidly, it may be imperative that the new Widget take priority over old Gizmo. If everything in the organization descends from one of these two objectives, it will be readily apparent if the organization is mistakenly prioritizing Gizmos over Widgets even if out of sheer inertia.

Having a sole individual own unrestricted objectives in an organization makes it easy to have frank conversations and track accountability. Leaves in the organization can raise issues to those to whom they are accountable. Those individuals can in-turn re-raise the issue to the person to who they are accountable. Eventually, every issue becomes part of someone's tracked work—tied into the objective hierarchy—or a decision is made and logged to not pursue an objective. The person who makes that decision is then accountable for the fall-out if it turns out to be a poor decision.

In this way, ownership is always coupled to accountability except at the very top of the organization chart. By coupling the two, we maintain a hierarchy of objectives that trace the chain of accountability from top-to-bottom of an organization. Each level in the org chart serves to translate the concerns of their direct reports into an account of how the business is pursuing the objective assigned to them. "Be ready to fly helicopters on a moment's notice," turns into, "Fly the helicopter every day and do the routine maintenance so they don't break down." The generals care that helicopters are ready for conflict at a moment's notice. The mechanics care about the logistics of maintenance. Everyone in between translates between the two viewpoints by successively reforming the objective they are given and know how to handle into an objective their reports can be given and know how to handle.

But the generals are playing with table-stakes. Their job is to be ready for anything that may reasonably happen, and "I'm sorry Mr. President, we cannot do that," is not acceptable. Their continued leadership depends upon their ability to be ready for war at a moment's notice.

In a similar vein: You cannot cancel a pandemic-response unit of the CDC and expect to still be prepared for a once in a lifetime pandemic. It's a table-stakes game and the function of government is, in part, to take resources from the people in order to manage the table-stakes risks we would all face otherwise.

Literal Accountability

English is a funny language because literal interpretations of words often lead to insight.

Accountability.

"Accountability."

"Account" "ability."

Account ability.

Taken literally: The ability to account for something.

It defines the triangular relationship between two people and an objective. Both have a vested interest in the objective, and one will account to the other for their actions with respect to the objective. The accountable party is ultimately the one who drives the objective forward at the behest of the individual who delegated it to them.

This may be a transitive delegation; one individual may make another individual accountable for an objective that they themselves are accountable for. In this case, one party provides an account to the next, and that individual shares the account with the owner of the objective.

For each objective, there is always exactly one individual who shoulders the accountability burden. One individual who can tell the account of how the objective was a success or failure. One individual who accounts for the outcome.

This may seem restrictive; that is intentional. By having just one individual shoulder the accountability for an objective, the individual is empowered to make decisions regarding the objective. Where they have questions or choices to make, they can consult with the individual that delegated to them. When the objective is complete, they provide an account of what happened in order to judge the work complete. That account flows up the organizational hierarchy, following the chain of accountability induced from the organization's objectives. Each individual is able to re-frame the account of what happened with respect to a broader objective that they've been made accountable for delivering.

In the event of an organizational failure, it becomes easy to get the right people to account for the failure. Every individual has the ability to account for their actions, and, therefore, can contribute to the overall picture of the failure. No one individual has the complete account; the story of what happened comes out in the individual accounts. By interviewing all people involved, a retrospective can be compiled that will be a reasonably complete and accurate report of the failure. Too often retrospectives are written by a single individual; history is full of stories from the party that didn't lose.

For that reason, an individual's ability to track and account for objectives provides strong evidence for their ability to work with and manage the work of others. Tracking and accounting for objectives requires a healthy amount of self-reflection and critical thinking. Some people have a natural talent for this; others have to work harder at it. An individual who can track and account for objectives can, usually, concisely summarize the reason behind a failure because they are able to frame it in terms of objectives.

Tracking work and objectives honestly requires a great deal of self-reflection. The ability to see that what one *actually did* matches *what one was supposed to do* is an essential skill that people lack all-too-often. People often move on auto-pilot, doing the next step in a pre-programmed, habitual way. San Francisco put up cross-walk buttons that clearly state, "Accessible message only," yet people regularly stand there pushing the button to get the cross-walk to work. People are, in the aggregate, creatures of habit.

Self-reflection and accountability aren't one-off actions, either. They are a continual, ongoing process that all individuals should use to engage with their work. Self-reflection makes for better accountability because one is accountable to oneself.

The ability to account for something.

Delegation

Delegation bridges the gap between ownership and accountability because unrestricted ownership must be exceptional.

When an individual is given an objective, they can break it down into several sub-objectives that collectively answer the call posed by the original objective. They are empowered to drop or reassign these objectives, so long as they account for it in the context of the original objective they are accountable for. They can then delegate these sub-objectives to other accountable parties.

This pattern of behavior, when repeated across the chain of command, will lead to a linked chain of accountability for objectives. A chain of delegates. At each level there is both accountability and ownership. As an owner they are empowered to accept the account of the person to whom they delegated work—or reject it and require changes. As an accountable party, they are required to provide an account for the work to the person to whom they account.

Through delegation the individuals set up a scenario to play out in which many transactional events lead to work getting done. The hierarchy implied by delegation is one-to-one with the objective hierarchy. Delegation naturally dovetails with the chain of command to provide a structure that brings forth this hierarchy. That's by design.

Each link in the chain converts accountability into ownership, and then possibly more accountability. Individuals capable of directing the work of others have a clear means by which to do so. Individuals capable of executing on vague or broad objectives can rise to the level of their capability and delegate work to other capable individuals.

Delegation and accountability are projections of the same structure. Delegation signals to the party that they will be accountable for the outcome in the future; they will be the one to provide the account of an objective in the annals of history.

Work flows down, an account of the work flows up. The delegated work brings with it the necessity to account for the work once it is done.

One implies the other.

Mutually arising opposites.

Accountability is to Someone

One consequence of the chain of accountability is that accountability in an organization is always to someone else.

The leader of the organization is accountable to society. And society is structured to bring accountability in the form of laws, journalism, and vigilante justice.

Two of those more than the third.

Everyone within the organization is accountable to the leader, usually through one or more managers, directors, VPs, or officers.

But always to someone.

In this way, delegation and accountability provide frames around the discussions people have about the organization's priorities and what the individual should prioritize. As new intelligence is gathered on the ground, it flows up the chain of accountable parties until someone captures it in an organization's objective. Responsibility for that objective then flows back down the hierarchy, realigning the priorities of people as it goes.

Accountability to someone else.

This is what makes the organization tick. Being explicit about accountability can literally make the organization run like clockwork because individuals can, at all times, know who to reach with important work; sometimes this will mean the important work is deemed not important. Nothing gets done faster than something that's explicitly out of scope.

Because accountability is always to someone else, it provides the framework for conversations about the business. Each objective should be the subject of regular conversations. Objectives and Key-Results shouldn't be discussed just at the start and end of the quarter, but should be part of an ongoing dialogue between the parties.

Responsibility is Shared

Responsibility derives from accountability.

The objectives for which one is directly accountable contribute to a broader objective for which one is partially responsible.

Responsibility is shared; accountability is not.

Therefore, responsibility is largely about monitoring resource allocation and providing attribution to work. It's a past-tense of the process that happens when an individual is accountable for an objective. They are responsible for the success or failure of a objective.

Responsibility itself is a nearly meaningless concept except in conjunction with ownership and accountability. A responsible party shares in the success and blame for an outcome. An accountable party shields from retribution those who are responsible for failure, while ensuring that rewards and praise are provided to all those responsible for success.

Defraying the responsibility for failure is a key aspect of managing morale in an organization. Individuals will be held to account for their individual objectives—sometimes at the cost of their relationship to the organization—but will generally be shielded by the organization for failure. An organization that punishes failure will find its people work to hide failure and deflect blame. An organization that naturally shields those responsible while holding individuals accountable by rewarding transparency is well-placed to succeed.

When failure strikes—as is expected on a long enough timeline—the root cause can be easily uncovered through mechanistic processing of the accounts for the work. Individuals who make contemporaneous accounts of the work they do, as well as the conversations they have, paint a picture of the way in which the organization failed to meet its objectives. An organization that rewards this kind of self-reflection is well-placed to learn from its mistakes and do better in the future.

Frank conversations about failure are equally healthy and uncomfortable; however, they are absolutely essential to the business.

Bottom-Up and Top-Down

It is said that an organization can be of one of two forms: Bottom-Up or Top-Down. In a top-down organization, the goals and objectives are specified from above. Organizational objectives percolate down to become objectives for individual contributors to the organization. In a bottom-up organization, new objectives originate in those closest to the concrete work of the organization and are guided by individuals above them in the org chart.

Trying to argue for one or the other misses the point.

In a healthy organization, priorities flow down from a position of visibility and long-term vision. There has to be someone consuming all signals of the organization and reflecting on them regularly. A building without a chief architect is likely to be schizophrenic in its presentation; different architects will express their position differently and the building will lack coherency. A restaurant without a head chef or other standard-bearer will suffer from the individualism of the cooks present.

Similarly, working decisions need to be made by those closest to the work. It is nearly impossible to specify something at the conversational level and have a sufficient meeting of the minds that the two people will be able to go separate directions and arrive at the same result. Regular, ongoing communication between people closest to the work is necessary, and a bottom-up organization is built around such communication.

The problem with a top-down organization is that people don't like being told what to do—and will often do the wrong thing as a matter of miscommunication. The problem with a bottom-up organization is that people will do as they please absent direction to the contrary; isn't such direction top-down?

The key observation to note is that top-down is a great way to set one's priorities, but a terrible way to schedule work; and bottom-up is a great way to schedule work, but a terrible way to dissuade people from bad decisions.

Both are essential to the health of an organization. Priorities should be aligned across the organization. That necessarily implies some form of a central nervous system; there's a reason humans can think better than jellyfish (a being that lacks a central nervous system). Every organization, whether top-down or bottom up needs a central nervous system at its core that can make decisions and stimulate the rest of the organization.

A good organization encodes something of a central nervous system, whether the organization is top-down or bottom up. Like a well-conditioned neuron, each vantage point in an organization needs to react consistently to the stimulus they are presented with for an organization to work. Each vantage point in an organization has to be trusted to make decisions at their level *and to escalate and delegate to others as necessary.*

Consistent thought. That's the key in leadership, no matter the direction. A good leader sets priorities in a consistent fashion, and consistent prioritization is the hallmark of a well-run top-down organization. Some *one* needs to be present to absorb the influx of signals and provide a consistent solution to the problems that rise to their level.

Consistency is key.

Chaos is hard to work with.

A chaotic leader is hard to follow.

A consistent leader naturally gains followers.

A consistent leader doesn't thrash the organization with changing processes. Priorities will change, but when problems are solved in a consistent fashion by leadership, the decisions of tomorrow will be more likely to align to the decisions of yesterday. A consistency in how the organization solves its problems will allow for better alignment and faster velocity because of reuse of intellectual capital.

A healthy organization needs intelligence and observations to flow upwards and priorities and direction to flow downwards. A healthy organization needs its people to align at all levels.

This alignment is easy with consistent leadership. If the organization was aligned yesterday, and takes every opportunity to stay aligned today, it will necessarily be aligned tomorrow. Do this daily, and the organization is inductively aligned forever.

An organization without top-down leadership will be out of alignment and will not move the entire organization fast. The success of D-Day wasn't in one or two teams moving fast in a bottom-up fashion. The success of D-Day was commanding a plurality of people—each with their own orders—to move in concert so well that it overwhelmed the enemy and allowed the Allies to take Normandy. Quickly landing just one boat would not have had the same effect; it was the ability to move 24,000 people at once, in concert, that lead to the success that day.

Once an organization becomes large enough, it necessarily must move slower to stay in sync, but because it is larger it will still have a larger net-effect than a smaller, more agile organization.

In a bottom-up organization, it is very likely that some teams move fast, and others move slow; then the organization as a whole wonders where the friction enters the system. Why can some teams move fast, but others are always moving slow? Sometimes its the fast-movers creating roadblocks and churn in the rest of the organization.

Top-down leadership is necessary to balance an organization from the perils of competition that arise with a bottom-up workflow.

A river that tries to flow everywhere will not flow with force.

You Can't Control Other People

"You can't control other people. So how do you get what you want?"

Most people know the answer right away.

Some people know the answer right away, but are hesitant to say it. It seems... wrong.

The answer is simple, obvious really. And yet, most people to whom I've posed this puzzle hesitate to provide the answer right away, although it is clear that they have the answer.

The know it.

They just won't say it.

Why is it that hard? The answer comes quickly, but people seem to seek a different answer.

Why should I expect differently of them? It's an established pattern, so should I expect any deviation from the pattern?

Clearly not.

People are hesitant to vocalize hard truths. And the answer to this puzzle is either obvious or uncomfortable depending on the individual providing an answer.

It's not a hard problem; so why haven't I given the answer?

For the sake of exposition.

And because it's what I'm going to do.

So, you can't control other people; how do you get what you want?

Want what they're going to do.

The Peter Principle

The Peter Principle says that people will rise to the level of their incompetence. It's an observation that people will eventually, in the limit, hit a wall where their skill set doesn't match the job. It's not a statement that organizations intentionally promote incompetent people. An individual either runs out of room to be promoted, or, more likely, rises to a position that requires skills they do not have.

There's buried implicit statement about the first $n - 1$ levels of competence before the *n*th level of incompetence. A person will rise through several levels where they are competent before they will not have the skills for the job at hand. In these levels, the individual is capable and has the skills to succeed. As they grow into their level, they observe the next-higher level. Observant individuals will pick up on their immediate superior's behavior and begin to replicate it in their own work. In this way, individuals demonstrate the ability to operate at the next level.

For this reason, organizations often promote from within, and only promote the individuals step-wise. The most fitting individual to rise into a role is selected—usually for demonstrating that they already have the skills necessary to succeed in both their old and new positions. In this way, an individual has the skill-set necessary to perform every duty that will fall underneath them; consequently, they are prepared to handle any situation that comes up under their jurisdiction.

This leaves talent on the table.

To be precise: People are a diverse crowd, and some people may have strong display of skills that presents asymmetrically. Especially for neurodiverse individuals, it's possible to have a strong set of strengths accompanied by a strong set of deficits. It may not be possible to cover all the skills hierarchically, and the deficits will eventually become a limiting factor. A good leader in this position—and the Peter Principle says most leaders will find themselves in this position—knows to surround themselves with more-capable people to do the heavy lifting. What matters is that they possess the ability to communicate clearly in order to align people who—transitively—do the work at the lower levels.

Thinking in strict terms of ownership, accountability, and responsibility can help bridge this gap for people with diverse brains. The clear method of thought prescribed by this exercise gives a concrete pattern of communication for extracting from those above and directing those below. Managers can work with the explicit ownership and accountability provided by the framework. The regular communication along the chain of accountability gives an individual practice communicating at a higher level.

In the context of the Peter Principle, we can now say something more about the rise to one's level of incompetence: A failure to succeed at one's level is a failure in the training provided by the organization. Leadership is about communication and strategy. If a leader isn't providing clear feedback regularly, the individual is left to self-reflect using, solely, the information available to them. Thinking about ownership, accountability, and responsibility in the ways discussed thus far gives an explicit means for practicing communication and learning strategy. Both develop from having explicit, focused discussions about the business at the next-higher level with those higher in the org chart.

This gives an opportunity for diverse talent: Some individuals may excel at creating project plans, having long-term vision, and following a North Star through the San Francisco fog. Managing people often requires a set of softer skills than managing the work to be done. It's for this reason that software engineering managers often pair with a tech lead to direct the technical solutions. This enables a person who cannot manage people to run a large project successfully; put another way, it enables a person who is less technical to run a large team successfully.

Explicit, directed communication is key. It's uncomfortable, but it maximizes the learning potential, which minimizes the risk of petering into a position where one does not succeed.

What's important is that individuals have conversations about the work they are responsible for in proportion to their responsibility. Many conversations at their next higher level with their lead. Always a level higher for the same reason most people work out with weights. Many conversations at their level with peers. Some conversations at two or three levels plus. Rare conversation at the top of the hierarchy. Learning to work with people up the org chart in a way that produces non-zero-sum effects.

Leverage

Good leadership means leading people.

This should not be a controversial position: Leaders definitionally have people follow them. In general, the extent to which one is capable of leading is heavily correlated with the number of people one leads. Put another way: A bad leader won't lead many people or for long. People can identify leaders that align to their values and will vote with their feet if there is no alignment. A good leader will retain and attract good people.

More people, more leverage.

Leverage.

That's the key to quantifying leadership potential.

Leverage is a multiplier on person-hours. It's the ability to put in more hours directly than one individual has to directly contribute by getting other people to put in *their* hours too. Each of these individuals has their own multiplier that contributes to the leader's multiplier.

Therefore, leverage is the ability to direct more person-hours than one can put in directly. It is the ability to get people to account for their working time in a way that creates a feedback loop. The more people one leads, the more cumulative time one person has influence over. The more time one can direct, the more leverage one can have, and the more one can successfully account for.

Good leadership will take advantage of this.

That's not to say that good leaders, when thinking about leverage, tell people what to do. It's quite the opposite: good leaders gain followers and leverage as one mutually-arising construction. A good leader will be able to stir people to action, and be able to succinctly communicate ideas.

We can measure leverage via the objective hierarchy. When an individual has more transitive reports, they have more leverage. With more leverage, an individual is able to direct larger objectives.

But leverage is lossy. Leading three individuals does not yield the work output of four people. There's an overhead that comes from managing other people. Overhead saps leverage. A good leader can reduce overhead by aligning their team to pull as one.

Alignment increases leverage. Headcount increases leverage.

Leverage is the product of alignment and headcount.

Video Games

The GameBoy seems designed for interrupted play. Many games are built such that the GameBoy can be set down at any time and the game keeps state until the user provides input. The original Pokémon games exemplify this with their menu-driven play style. At any time you can take your focus off the GameBoy and nothing bad happens. Usually nothing at all happens.

Play; set down; play some more.

It's a very instruction-driven play style. The game simply plays until it needs to await the next instruction from the player. With a little play, the gamer gets to the point where they can reasonably predict what pause points they can take, which they need to explicitly pause for, and when they need to keep playing.

Play; set down; play some more.

GameBoy games can tell us quite a bit about planning, prioritization, and urgency. Games like the original Pokémon are time-invariant, requiring no regular input. So long as the game remains on, the user can set it down or proceed slowly. Such a process is truly able to sit for long periods of time, and no amount of waiting will make it accumulate work. Waiting will leave work undone, but work will not accumulate.

Games like those in the Super Mario World platformer series are time-sensitive and require regular attention to keep the game going. If the user sets the game down without explicitly pausing it, they will likely suffer a loss in the game. Such a process will accrue debt or loss if left to run without regular interaction.

These two game styles highlight a spectrum between time-invariant and time-sensitive games as a metaphor for time-invariant and time-sensitive objectives. Something time-invariant doesn't require regular tending. It happens of itself. Only when the player wants to change course does it require input or change. Something time-sensitive requires regular tending. When choosing which to emulate in the interactions between individuals of an organization, we should prefer time-invariant processes; something akin to multiple planes putting in bearings on autopilot through parallel tracts across the Atlantic Ocean.

Back to the GameBoy: We should learn to present our information via time-insensitive means. Too many apps demand instant attention with notifications; instant gratification. Communication being instant tends to reward this ability to reach into a coworker's space and ding-ding your way to their attention. Instead of being in need of constant attention, sit idly until the time comes for the user to check the app. Communication that is written in anticipation of such a delay will be inherently more detailed—if you have to wait for an answer, you'll likely include more context, more detail, and more of what you considered before pressing "send".

Treating objectives like a video game goes both ways: If the app rewards time-insensitive means properly, it doesn't just encourage people to write thoughtful work-product, but it also presents the consumer of information with a time-invariant way to process the communication. By encouraging time-invariancy, we can allow the leaders of the organization to serve as interrupt handlers that, ironically, can provide better service than time-sensitive communication affords because people bother to put all the back-and-forth in one iteration, and leadership can prioritize the message of most importance rather than being bombarded with a notification for each inbound request.

The app people spend their day in—and email works well here—should encourage a standard of behavior that renders most systems time-invariant to the people one level removed from the system's place in the org chart.

Alignment

It's interesting how small levels of misalignment can yield big losses to an organization.

This can be illustrated by way of metaphor: Walk the Land's End trail of San Francisco and it'll take some number of hours to complete. Walk the trail by ping-ponging back and forth between the trails edges in a sinusoidal fashion—a metaphor for misalignment—and it'll take significantly more time to complete.

How much more? Seven to eight times longer than walking the trail directly. Never more than one unit away from the center of the trail, and yet nearly eight fold longer.

Small misalignments can contribute to major slowdowns.

Imagine the same forces of misalignment at work in an organization. There's a reason that people who grow an organization experience growing pains: As people become even slightly misaligned, it contributes to a non-linear slowdown in their work and priorities.

Correcting misalignment takes a dedicated individual who can, first, recognize that there's misalignment between their goal and someone else, and, second, convince others of the need to change to become aligned on the greater good for society.

Building alignment requires recognition and conversation.

Or a type system...

OKRs

There's a framework I learned at my first software engineering role called Objectives and Key-Results. It was developed by Andrew Grove while he was at Intel. It's the goal, plus the quantifiable outcomes that can be used to judge the results as complete or partially complete.

I never understood the relationship between objectives and key results except to say that there's a relationship between them. What I witnessed was that objectives at the team level turned into key results as part of a broader objective at the director level. The two were rarely written in the same language and sometimes didn't even have the same meaning to me. In at least one instance, the quantifiable measurements didn't even contain numbers of the same order of magnitude. Alignment seems impossible in light of these anomalies.

To me, a recursive objective—as we've explored thus far—gives a way of consistently specifying objectives and key-results. Each objective has several sub-objectives, some of which would qualify as key results. In this way, one person's key-result is—directly—someone else's objective. There may be sub-objectives that are not quantifiable—maybe just binary deliverables; these may not meet the definition of a key-result, but may still be necessary.

Framed in this fashion, every objective—and we use the term "objective" as a catch-all to capture the notion of milestones, waypoints, tasks, stories, epics, key-results, and objectives—gives a framework for people to focus on their work. There is no need to distinguish the type of an objective; it should be just a plain language description of the work that allows for determining when the work is complete and can be forgotten.

Agile Means Change

Agile work processes—all the rage in tech companies—mean that objectives will have to change.

In the old days, people followed a waterfall method of planning wherein each stage of the planning was completed before moving onto the next stage. This has the risk of encountering insurmountable problems late in the development stage that would reset the waterfall.

I imagine that to counter this, much of the work that looks like planning was actually about doing the engineering work in a planning document prior to doing the actual engineering. Waterfall's not our goal, so I'll leave it to others to discuss the merits of waterfall in comparison to agile methods.

Agile methods center around change: The core tenant of agile is that what you work on can change relatively rapidly to accommodate external stimulus to the planning process and new discoveries.

Continual refinement.

That's what agile brings to the table.

With an agile process—and this is a generalization—objectives change regularly in light of new information. In our objective hierarchy, this should manifest as changes toward the leaves with gradual adjustments up the hierarchy. There's an inverse proportionality between the size of the objective and how much it can change without thrashing its sub-objectives.

This gives us a way to use agile processes to plan in a top-down manner. What starts as a big objective high up in the org chart gets refined with those directly responsible for it. These individuals recursively run a tentative planning process on the objectives they would be responsible for if the objectives were finalized. As the objectives at the top become more solidified, the people responsible have a clearer idea of where their own objectives and planning processes sit with respect to the organization. Depending on the size of the objective and the working styles of all involved, there's no reason an organization cannot run multiple tiers of this planning process in parallel.

People at the leaves will see more thrashing about during this process, so it's imperative to position this work as a planning exercise rather than actual work to be done. Their contribution to the work is to provide sufficiently detailed objectives that *could* be completed to give a picture of the true costs involved in the plan. In this way all individuals in an organization contribute to the planning process and feel a sense of control over their destiny.

Meetings

It's common advice to state that every meeting should have an agenda; put another way, every meeting should have an objective. Ideally this would be an objective that's aligned to the objectives of the organization; even better, the agenda should be a link to an objective that will be discussed. A well-specified objective dictates the agenda.

The question, then, becomes who should be invited to a well-specified meeting.

We can answer this question by looking to the structure of people related to the objective.

First and foremost, the person who is most accountable for the objective that defines the agenda should be in attendance as the meeting coordinator.

Then, the person to whom the meeting coordinator is accountable should be invited to the meetings; they have a vested interest in seeing the objective match their own objectives and a meeting gives a high-bandwidth way to align all individuals in attendance. If they decline to attend, they elect to consume the meeting via the notes taken by someone in attendance. A meeting they don't care to attend or hear about after the fact is likely misaligned with respect to the organization's objectives, or is a frivolous meeting that should be canceled.

Next on the attendance list should be the individuals directly responsible for the objective on the agenda. These individuals are accountable for the objectives owned by the meeting coordinator. These individuals use the meeting to align their actions and sub-objectives to the parent objective under discussion.

Lastly on the invite list should be people who function as consultants to the meeting. These individuals do not own any objective under discussion, but instead have domain expertise that contributes to the meeting in order to help align individuals.

In short, a well-scoped meeting has as its main focus one or more related objectives and will include those responsible and accountable for the objectives, as well as an optional representative of the person who owns the objective under discussion.

Like with the objective hierarchy, these simple rules can be mechanically verified. This verification can be used to suggest which meetings to decline, which people to invite or dis-invite, and what objectives are the most time-consuming.

Email

There's a tendency in modern organizations to behave as if instant communication at all times means the organization is communicating—and by extension, operating—well.

This is a misplaced idea.

Instant messenger is wonderful for encouraging people to talk, but terrible for encouraging actual communication.

For starters, a conversation that everyone must follow in its entirety in order to remain up-to-date with their co-workers is an efficiency nightmare. Even if everyone contributes just one message per conversation, the resulting discussion requires everyone to read everyone else's message. As the number of people in an organization grows, the total number of messages read grows quadratically. It just doesn't scale.

Of course, most communication tools have multiple "channels" or "forums" in which an individual can reside, so the communication is tailored to the audience and objectives. So long as communication happens in the right channel, people can stay up-to-date without parsing through the entirety of the organizations' message history. Unfortunately, many organizations do their instant messaging in closed channels, making it hard for an individual who is not a member in the channel to follow what's going on.

This is the second terrible property of instant-messaging: Channels require discoverability. For example, many apps have a feature that lets an individual discover which channels other people like them are also in; never-mind that this will only introduce them to people they already know.

Discovering other channels has at its core the assumption that an individual knows what they are looking for. Finding the right channel to talk about something is synonymous with knowing which nouns or verbs one needs to search for to find the right audience: Once in the right channel, the individual has the appropriate audience for their inquiries.

With an objective hierarchy, we already have our discoverability mechanism: The work assigned to an individual becomes the means by which the communication about that work is grouped. Pick the audience based upon the objective at play and let the messaging platform disseminate upwards for accountability and downwards to those responsible for the objective. Given the objective, finding the right people is trivial. Further, following the links of the hierarchy increases the chances of discovering a broader audience with a vested interest in helping the work succeed.

Surprisingly, tech firms have given up on one of the core technologies of the Internet that is perfectly suited for this pattern of communication: email. Email provides contemporaneous notes of everything involved to those who are directly involved in the communication, and allows others to be brought into the chain by adding them to the CC. Work can be delegated by forwarding the message or adding someone to the CC line. Decisions can be documented by sending a summary of the decision thread to a decisions@ list. People can surface the email to those to whom they are accountable using with a simple message. There's no need for an added application to facilitate communication. The objectives of the organization can even be tied to email aliases for all involved to subscribe.

This sounds like a trivial point, but tools meant for communication often miss the point: Instead of enabling communication, they—relative to what's possible in a free-form format—constrain what can be done. Worse, every new mode of communication, every new way of interacting has to be affirmatively enabled through new features. And no matter how restrictive a tool becomes, people will find ways of circumventing conventions of the tool to enforce their own conventions.

Email starts by permitting everything and then scoping down

what's possible through individual discipline.

I once took a position where I envisioned, hoped really, to work entirely from email. It was something of a crazy dream, but I saw a world in which every type of communication was possible via email. I would take on work via email, and document my work to others via email. It would be relatively simple to split my time between email and the terminal, and I would be known for working via email.

Instead, what I've discovered is that people are forced into modes of working from a variety of applications that constantly tell us how to work. Every workplace interaction I had in the week prior to writing this chapter could be done over email with templates and status updates. Further, it would be more discoverable, more centralized, and easier for others to stay in-sync with me. With a tool like Slack or Jira, you are at the mercy of the tool's authors to have imagined your use case and written code to enable it; with email you are at the mercy of your ability to craft a message articulating your point—the computer stays out of the way.

We're progressively working toward having every mode of interaction regulated by the computer systems to which we subject ourselves. Every new thing we want to do requires effort from some company elsewhere in the digital world to "enable" behavior.

There's a reason that whiteboards and paper reign supreme for people sketching ideas ideas compared to more rigid tools: They permit the individual to make exceptions to the rules where, in their better judgment, they want to deviate from convention. What the apps do well is provide a framework for filling in form fields; unfortunately a free-form comment or text box provides no guidance for how to fill it in.

If you're going to make use of free-form text, why not use the ultimate in free-form text?

Why not shed the baggage and cut out the middle-app?

I hypothesize that the objective hierarchy of an organization provides better guidance than any tool I've used for coordinating work. The individuals directly related to an objective—that is, the owner of an objective, the accountability chain for the objective, and the responsible individuals—must all be informed of developments in the objective. We can capture this in a tool for facilitating work-tracking and communication. The tool captures organizational objectives for work tracking provides a stable email alias to write concerning each objective. This stable email alias fulfills the same role as a topic or channel in other platforms, but has one key benefit: It integrates with the tool these other tools ultimately fall-back on for distributing notifications about in-app activity.

Using these dynamic lists enables communication to match the objective hierarchy, and by extension, the org chart. People accountable for an objective are listed as responsible for the objective from which their objective descends; they are on both lists and make the effort to shuffle knowledge from one list to the other, translating to the audience of each list. We rely upon the individual judgment the organization pays for in order to non-mechanically communicate changes in status and outcome. It doesn't take any longer to write an email summarizing the disposition of an objective than it does to comment in a work-tracking tool and then transition the work to the "done" state.

This is an intentional simplification of what tools already do: Every interaction with the web UI in a tool like Jira has the potential to send an email. Every slack message sent when an individual is offline gets turned into an email. Google drive sends a new email *and* a new slack message each time someone interacts with a document.

We've already collectively decided that email is a necessary part of our workflow.

Why not simplify things and cut out the middle-app?

Cadence

Every process goes on until it ends.

That's the nature of process after all.

And organizations are about building process.

Process is predictable and repeatable. By framing organizational activity as a set of processes, we can describe what the organization has a habit and history of doing in a repeatable way. In most organizations, organizational activity can be framed in terms of processes over the objective hierarchy. It's rare to find an objective that cannot be framed as part of an ongoing process of the organization, because there will always be broad categories of processes for maintaining course.

In the limit, what we want to do is specify objectives that represent process as ongoing objectives in the system. This gives rise to the notion of a template objective. A template objective gets instantiated for each iteration of the process. A template objective encodes within it a means of specifying the state machine or flow chart for a process. Each instantiation of the template tracks the state machine to completion by creating sub-objectives automatically as the process unfolds.

The person or persons establishing a process should put into place the guardrails and recurring actions necessary to perpetuate the process using template objectives. They'll specify template objectives that get instantiated at the start of each iteration of the process. These objectives should serve as the recurring actions of the process, and well-defined actions and thorough documentation provides the guardrails.

In this way, much of a company can be cast as a set of processes that keep the company growing. Don't write software; build a process for writing software. Don't write a book; establish a writing discipline that generates books. Don't speculate about what the helicopter needs; fly it regularly and keep it in working order.

Everything that needs doing gets done with a particular cadence. New objectives from the leader get transformed from a vague process that runs at the top level to a concrete process somewhere lower in the hierarchy. That concrete process then turns into a set of discrete objectives.

The cadence of the organization as a whole will ebb and flow. Some days or weeks will see a surplus of objectives become scheduled simultaneously. Some days will experience the opposite phenomenon and a corresponding decrease in the number of scheduled objectives.

Computers can help mitigate this phenomenon.

By scheduling recurring objectives in a careful manner, a computer can ease the ebb and flow of background objectives to give the business a predictable baseline of productivity that's necessary to service the processes it has already committed to.

Enter the Type System

Thus far, we've explored objectives in the abstract; maybe with some examples.

Now, we will get concrete in our definitions such that a vital property emerges: We can mechanically verify an organization's objectives, structure, and communication patterns to paint a picture of organizational health. The property we want is that an organization that we deem to be healthy is more able to adapt and take on new work than a less-healthy organization.

Axiomatically, an organization is deemed to be in alignment when all individuals act in aligned ways. For the computer, it's about aligning the objectives and priorities of an organization mechanistically so that individuals within the organization know that they are moving in the same way as their co-workers.

This is the property we want to uphold: If every individual makes sure that the translation from work they are accountable for to work they own is in alignment, the organization as a whole must be in alignment *and a computer can verify this alignment across the organization.*

In software, we call this mechanical verification "static analysis." When a program is well-formed, static analysis serves as a proof that certain, basic properties are upheld. When a program fails to pass static analysis, the programmer gets informed of the problem as soon as it's discovered. For an organization, this would mean controls in-place to prevent people from making objectives or scheduling meetings not aligned to the organization's need.

Organizational static analysis confers several benefits that are worth exploring: First, static analysis makes sure that all work is transitively tied to work owned by a single individual within the organization—usually the CEO. Second, static analysis gives insight into the organization's prioritization and planning; what people choose to work on paints a picture of their prioritization. Third, static analysis and the logged history of objectives paints a clear picture of the effective working relationships people have in order to facilitate organizational restructuring. Finally, static analysis can be used to infer automatic, ephemeral communication channels that last as long as the work lasts.

An organization that passes such static analysis will be inherently more able to adapt and take on new work because—and this is key—every new work item is verified to maintain the invariants necessary for good health.

This has the net effect of tying all work to a single individual's vision, as laid out in their objectives, that everyone in the company is predisposed to follow in their own work. Everyone can clearly see how their work relates to big, company-wide goals. Everyone can clearly see how work transforms from vision to practice. Similarly, the way this individual prioritizes work can percolate down the chains of accountability to give people a clear view of how important an objective is.

These properties ensure that an organization only passes static analysis to the degree it is in alignment.

Rules for the Type System

The rigid way in which we've defined the notions of ownership, accountability, and responsibility leads us to a very strong property: It becomes possible to check the health of the organization programmatically in a principled way. We can check that all objectives tie into objectives of the business. That is, for each objective, there is a single chain of accountability wherein each individual directly delegates an objective, or breaks the objective into smaller objectives, which are then delegated.

Assuming software can read the metadata for objectives—who owns it, who delegated it, etc.—the computer can check these chains of accountability and provide the individual with the ways in which their work matters to the business.

The computer enforces three rules: First, every objective must have an owner. Second, if an objective's owner is not the leader of the organization, the objective must have a parent objective for which the owner of the objective is directly accountable. Third, every objective has a single actively accountable party, which defaults to the owner. These rules create a linked hierarchy of objectives. Each objective necessarily has a single root that flows up all the way to the leader, enabling leadership to guide the direction of the company without micro-managing work. These rules shouldn't be surprising—they've been the rules we've been following for this whole book.

Asserting that these three rules hold for every objective in an organization is sufficient to prove that local alignment—each individual's assertion that the objectives they create directly relate to the work they're accountable for—will lead to global alignment. The proof of this is simple: Assume that everyone is locally aligned, but not globally aligned. This implies that there must be some pair of individuals who are misaligned. If they belong to the same singular accountability chain, then somewhere in that chain the misalignment happens within an individual, violating our assumption that they are locally aligned. If the pair of individuals belong to different accountability chains that merge, there must be a misalignment within the path way between the two individuals. Only if the accountability chains are totally distinct will it be possible to diverge globally without diverging locally. The second rule of static analysis ensures that there cannot be two distinct leaders of the organization.

Static analysis of the objective hierarchy has several implications for ownership and accountability. The only person who can drop an objective without accounting for it is the leader of the organization. Everyone else's objectives have a parent objective whose owner receives an account of the dropped objective. Lower in the org chart, every objective has a parent, so this check will always involved a reason for dropping the objective, and an email message accounting for progress to the parent objective's owner.

Under this framework, there are two actions an individual accountable for an objective can take: An individual can abdicate or finish the objective, explicitly giving the objective back to the person who delegated it to them; or an individual can sub-delegate an objective to another individual. Moving accountability for an objective from one individual to another is the composition of these two actions.

Finally, the rules for meeting attendance give us the ability to create dynamic communication channels for each objective. A transient email list. An email list with membership that grows as people become accountable for pieces of the objective. One channel per objective, with the person owns the objective, the delegated chain of people accountable for the objective, and the people responsible for the objective.

By having a single communication channel per objective—and email fits the bill here—we ensure that the manual steps of static analysis have a home in which to thrive. Individuals can make use of the email list for an objective to ask clarifying questions, and leadership can use the channels for voicing alignment at their level.

This "dynamic analysis" should always be done with a human touch. The individual is accountable for making sure their owned objectives align to the parent objective in light of everything they know. This task should be done by someone capable of thinking and asking questions. An individual who makes a change to the objective hierarchy can immediately know that, if their local thought process was good, the global alignment of the organization holds.

Prioritization

Prioritization: It's what needs to get done first.

Prioritized: It's what was chosen during past prioritization.

The patterns of people's behavior specifies the effective priorities of the organization, both in the present and past tenses. Not the declared priorities, but the actual priorities. What people choose to do is what they prioritize. What an organization collectively chooses to do is what it prioritizes.

It's about choice of action.

One observation to make about prioritization is that it forms a partial order across objectives. Any two objectives either have a relative order between them, or they don't; and there are no cycles of priority in the organization's priorities. The partial order allows individuals to compare any two objectives and say their relative order, if one exists.

With two rules, we can run static analysis on an organizations priorities: First, the system must be complete; every objective has a priority. An objective that is most urgent has as its priority 0. Higher numbers indicate lower priority. This allows one to create "holes" in the priority scale to make room for new objectives by incrementing every objective with a priority equal to or greater than the desired hole, much like Hilbert's Hotel.

Second, the prioritization up a chain of accountability must be monotonically decreasing. An objective cannot be less urgent than the objective it descends from. If something is a p0 objective, it shouldn't be satisfied with a p∞ objective.

With these two rules satisfied, we can check that, at all times the priorities of the business are clear to all involved *and* individuals have a clear picture about how their assigned priorities contribute to the business.

An individual with two (or more) competing objectives, but only the budget to satisfy some of them escalates to the person or persons to whom they are accountable. If these individuals cannot come to an agreement on relative prioritization, they escalate up the chain of accountability. Eventually, they will reach individuals who can agree on the relative importance of the items to the organization, or a single individual who has is accountable for all objectives being escalated.

In this way, competing objectives always resolve into a total order when they conflict.

Static analysis, then, allows us to check that these orderings are maintained with each and every change. Consequently, it becomes possible to build tools that reveal the organization's true priorities. Such a tool can report on any discrepancy between the stated priorities and the order in which work gets completed. But with some additions, we can make the static analysis be useful for forward-looking prioritization which is sometimes spelled, "planning."

If we assign a relative size to each objective, something relatively abstract but also intuitive, we can measure and report on the work remaining to satisfy any given objective. One such scale would be t-shirt sizes where an XXXL t-shirt is an unbounded, unsized amount of work, and an XS t-shirt is at most a day of work. In between we can size things at the half, quarter, sprint, and smaller levels to give an approximate size estimate of the work. Notably, an objective estimated to take a quarter has much more variability than an objective estimated to take less than one day.

Planning is then the assignment of scale estimates to work; something that happens bottom-up. The plan becomes an estimate of the amount of work involved in getting an objective across the finish line.

We can apply rules similar to those used for prioritization to statically check planning: First, every objective must be assigned an estimate, and second, an objective cannot be specified to take longer than its parent objective. It can be the same size as the parent, or broken up into multiple t-shirts of the same size as the parent, but a single unit of work should never exceed the container objective within which it resides.

From these rules we can easily see where to allocate effort when planning. If a quarter-long objective is estimated to require four 4-four week objectives, the objectives must necessarily be scheduled concurrently. It's clearly an impossible situation setup for failure to assign all sixteen weeks to one person with the expectation that they complete them within twelve weeks. Such budgeting constraints can be easily verified with static analysis to say whether an objective hierarchy represents a viable path to success.

By applying static analysis to prioritizing and planning, it becomes possible to mechanically verify that it is possible for an organization to meet its objectives. Furthermore, with a bit of practice and tooling, it becomes possible to assign a probability of success to different objectives—a value that grows more uncertain as objectives are less of a priority.

The Org. Chart

The structure of the objective hierarchy leads to one very important property: We can induce the organization's effective org chart from the way in which accountability flows through the organization's members in practice.

When our rules for static analysis are upheld, every objective has a chain of objectives that terminate at a leader for the organization. They may have many such chains, indicating multiple paths through the leadership. The chain of objectives inducing a chain of people.

We can, then, recast the objective hierarchy as a form of an org chart, with people reporting to the people who delegate the work to them. Individuals with more than one party delegating work to them get assigned based upon organizational policy. Perhaps they report to the individual who assigns them the most work; more likely they should report to the lowest-ranking individual common to all the chains of accountability they participate in. If there is no such individual, the organization is split-brained and unlikely to be able to move fast.

This method of specifying the org chart ensures that individuals report to the individual most likely to hold them to account for their actions and to whom they would be able to provide the most value. This helps improve organizational retrospectives, and also reduces the tension that comes into play when an individual is caught between several competing interests. With just one individual to report to, each individual has a clear mind about their priorities.

Not a Cudgel

Static analysis is about an organization or project's structure. It's not about finding new ways to quantify individual productivity. An individual in a healthy organization will naturally fall into line and make progress on their assigned objectives.

If the static analysis were to be used for measuring individual productivity, people would, in addition to feeling micro-managed, begin to gamify their activity.

By keeping the reporting and tooling about the organization as a whole, an organization maintains its health without sacrificing the health of its employees. To encourage individuals to prioritize and plan honestly within the tooling requires an implicit contract that plans and priorities will not be used to cudgel individuals for failing to meet their plans. A project that never fails is not sufficiently ambitious for most contexts, nor is it honest about the failure it encounters along the way; individuals should be encouraged to take risks, so long as the risks routinely pay out. And individuals should be encouraged to call out failure, so long as they learn from it. Punishing failure leads individuals to hide failure.

The rules laid out for the objective hierarchy give individuals the framework within which to take calculated risks. Delivering a single project with 99% confidence is a different kind of working mode than delivering several projects with 25% confidence each. The overall payout could be the same for the organization, but some individuals will be more likely to succeed in one mode rather than the other. Some people are good at taking on risky work, and some people are good at planning out work to a high success threshold in accordance with long-term vision. In most organizations there is room for both modes of working.

Rust

The inspiration for the static analysis we've been exploring is the Rust programming language's borrow-checker. In short, the borrow checker upholds the following invariant: A value can be referenced with a single mutable reference or several immutable references, but never both at the same time.

Accountability is like holding a mutable reference in Rust. The holder of the reference can delegate it to another location, but cannot do anything with the reference until that delegation is over. Similarly, that delegation must come to an end, because the reference is borrowed, not owned. At the end of scope, it must be returned from where it was delegated, which means it must be returned to be returned.

Responsibility is like holding an immutable reference in Rust. The holder of the reference can make new objects that descend from it and include their own immutable reference, but the immutable reference says they should not do anything to change the reference they borrowed, except in narrow and well-defined ways.

Finally, ownership matches cleanly to Rust's ownership model. In Rust, only an owner can move an object to somewhere else, and only an owner can drop the object. If no one else has a reference to an object, the owner can always obtain a mutable or immutable reference to the object.

To complete the metaphor, the pattern of Rust code most closely aligned to our model is one in which the delegate of a mutable reference converts it to several immutable references, embeds each within a sub-objective, and then passes mutable references to these sub-objectives to their subordinates. The rules work for objects and objectives.

Fin

This book provides an intentionally simple framework for discussing ownership, accountability, and responsibility. Save for differences in the verbiage, it can directly map onto nearly any working style that people have because it is minimally prescriptive. It isn't meant to be a complete system that specifies the working structure of individuals; that would be too much like the applications that try to be the end-all-be-all of productivity management. Such tools are plentiful and have their purpose.

Instead, this book explores a view of the world that can be readily adopted within existing tooling and processes. Conversations around accountability and responsibility are often difficult—especially if the individuals have different backgrounds. Framing the conversation in terms of objectives, accountability, and the work as both parties see it has a clarifying effect that will make conversations easier for the individuals involved.

Individuals who have read this book are empowered to put it into practice immediately in their local work. Thinking explicitly about ownership, accountability, and responsibility can clarify one's own relationship to a business and give a good framework for figuring out what matters. Independent contributors without direct reports can immediately begin to think of the ways in which they are accountable to their higher-ups. People with direct reports can view themselves as the translator between higher-level priorities and the objectives they hold their reports accountable for delivering.

In short, the point of this book is to enable global leadership through local decisions and action. Every proposal in this book operates locally on each objective and globally on the objective hierarchy. This gives individuals a way to think about global impact in their local decisions. And when everyone is thinking about the same global impact to achieve in their actions, it becomes easy to align and work together.

Consequently, this chapter is not the end of a book, but the beginning of an ongoing conversation.

Made in the USA
Monee, IL
04 November 2026

67379956R00036